NORWICH
THEN and NOW

Philip Standley

Photography
Terry Burchell

John Nickalls Publications

Previous Titles (Philip Standley)
Norwich in Old Picture Postcards Volumes 1, 2, 3 and 4

First published in 2001 by John Nickalls Publications
First Reprint 2001
Second Reprint 2003
Oak Farm Bungalow, Sawyers Lane, Suton,
Wymondham, Norfolk, NR18 9SH
Telephone/Fax: 01953 601893

© 2001 Philip Standley
The moral right of the author has been asserted

ISBN 1 904136 01 X

Typeset by JEM Editorial, JEMedit@AOL.com

Printed by Geo. R. Reeve Ltd.
9-11 Town Green, Wymondham,
Norfolk, NR18 0BD
Telephone: 01953 602297

INTRODUCTION

Norwich has seen many changes over the years, and here I try to show a few of these with the help of postcards from my own collection. During the early part of the century road scenes, fires, floods and major events were all recorded on postcards. Norwich suffered severe damage by enemy bombing in the Second World War, hence the start of a massive rebuilding programme, which is still going on today.

Further changes will be taking place in Norwich in the near future, with the completion of the new library and the riverside development. The Nestlé factory site is to be redeveloped and there will be housing on the old Norfolk and Norwich Hospital site.

Philip Standley

ACKNOWLEDGMENTS

I am indebted to Rhoda Bunn, George Gosling and Basil Gowen for allowing me to use their postcards, also to Mike Sparkes for his help. Also, I thank most sincerely Terry Burchell for his brilliant photographic work and patience. He risked both life and limb to get the right angle for some of the pictures, and was often hindered by roadworks and construction work.

HAYMARKET, NORWICH. (319)

G.1660.

THEN – THE HAYMARKET _c_1935: This was the scene at the junction of The Haymarket with Brigg Street and Orford Place. On the left is the fine old shop front of Montague Burton, where suits were on offer for 37/- (£1.85). To the right is the Haymarket Cinema, which opened in 1911 and was enlarged in 1921 and 1929.

NOW: The cinema, and Burtons, were demolished in 1959 to make way for a modern shopping centre. The development had its orgins in the 1946 City Plan, which also saw conversion of the small garden that surrounded the statue of Sir Thomas Browne to a paved area with fountains of cascading water. The fountains have now been removed.

MARKET PLACE NORWICH

THEN – THE MARKET PLACE *c*1931: The view is from Gentleman's Walk. The stalls were bordered by the old municipal buildings, the Guildhall and the grand shop fronts of Dean and Palmer, tailors; Ellison's, tobacconist; and Chamberlins, the well-remembered outfitters, house furnishers and undertakers.

NOW: The only main feature which has not changed is the fifteenth century Guildhall. Gone are the municipal buildings in the wake of the redevelopment scheme of the 1930s, which included the new City Hall, the Garden of Remembrance and the widening of five streets. The statue of the Duke of Wellington, erected in the 1850s, was moved to Cathedral Close in 1937.

THEN – THE WALK: The picture is from shortly after the Second World War; public shelter signs can still clearly be seen in the foreground. The street gained its name from the bucks who, in Regency days, perambulated its length. For many years this was the main shopping street of Norwich.

NOW: Office blocks and new developments have changed the scene in the last fifty years, but as then, the magnificent church of St Peter Mancroft dominates the view. Today the market enjoys the advantage of a fixed position, and most of the area has become pedestrianised.

THE GUILDHALL NORWICH.

THEN – THE GUILDHALL *c*1910: This roadway, which connects St Giles and London Street, was known as Gaol Hill after the city gaol set back in the courtyard to the right, where the Norfolk and Norwich Subscription Library opened in its stead in 1835. The roadway to the left had the same name, as both hills were regarded as one. A century ago the right hand road became Guildhall Hill, leaving Gaol Hill on the 'wrong side'.

NOW: Above the modern shop fronts the Regency and early Victorian frontages may still be seen. The old thoroughfare has lost its tramway and is now a busy pedestrianised area, while Gaol Hill, to the left, has become a one-way street and taxi rank.

London Street, Norwich

THEN – LONDON STREET *c*1914: Before this street gained its popularity for its quality shops it was known as Cockey Lane after the open stream of water which ran along its length. At the top on the right was Jarrolds, the booksellers, binders, stationers and fancy goods shop, and at number 7 George Skipper, architect of many of the city's great buildings, had his offices. In the foreground the Norwich 'institutions' of drapers, Garland's, and silk mercers, Caley's, may be seen.

NOW: Once two-way, London Street was one of the first in the city to be fully pedestrianised. Many of the shops have been redeveloped and modern frontages have kept pace with the times. Garland's department store suffered a catastrophic fire in 1970 and, although rebuilt over the following years, was never quite the same, and the store closed for a final time in 1984. Afterwards the building was divided into smaller units.

THEN – LONDON STREET *c*1903: The view is from the corner of Castle Street, towards the Cathedral. Quality shops were set up around this area as an 'overspill' of the city centre in the nineteenth century. The street's name was also changed during this time from Cockey Lane to Little London Street, to reflect the growing affluence of the shops along its length. The shops' magnificent frontages were indicative of the prosperous Victorian age.

NOW: Still an area of good quality shops, London Street has been paved over and harks back to an even more distant time when Norwich was described as 'a city in a garden'. Along this busy shopping street trees have been planted and many of the shops are decorated with hanging baskets. Visitors to the cafés may dine *alfresco* in the summer months alongside the ice cream cart. In the winter the cart is replaced by one selling hot chestnuts. Colour and spectacle may be found here throughout the year as London Street enjoys many of the city's best street entertainers and buskers.

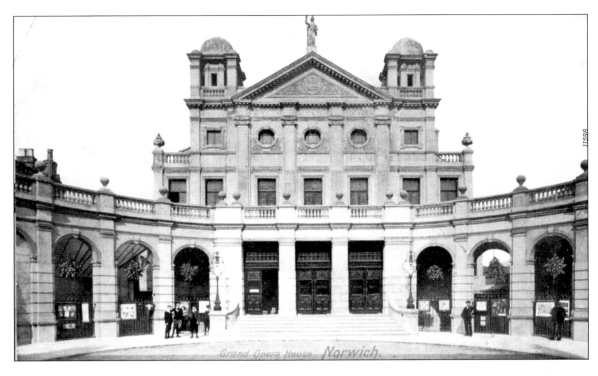

THEN – THE GRAND OPERA HOUSE: Financed by local entrepreneurs Bostock and Fitt, the Opera House was built in the Renaissance style in 1903 to seat 2,000. Some time later it became the Hippodrome and here some of the earliest bioscope films in the country were seen, as well as performances from such entertainers as Tommy Trinder, Henry Hall, Max Miller and Gracie Fields.

NOW: After a short spell as the unsuccessful Norfolk Playhouse, the Opera House/Hippodrome closed in 1960. It remained empty until 1966 when the decision was taken to demolish the building along with adjoining premises to make way for the St Giles Street car park.

THEN – BETHEL STREET *c*1912: This view looks towards St Giles Street. Centre stage is the charming shop front of George Bacon, the baker. Nearest on the right is the headquarters of the 2nd East Anglian Field Ambulance which, at the time, was under the command of Lt Col John Herbert Stacy, surgeon, medical officer and public vaccinator of Norwich.

NOW: The march of soldiers' feet are now a distant memory on Bethel Street; the field ambulance headquarters is now The Green House, a centre for ecologically-based organisations. The buildings to the left have been lost through blitz and demolition, but still standing today is the fine old hostelry, the Coach and Horses.

THEN – WELLINGTON LANE: This view of *c*1912 looks down Wellington Lane from St Giles Street to Pottergate. The lane is typical of the narrow, ancient streets that twisted and turned within the old city walls well into the twentieth century. Then, the city's population was around 25,000. Most of the people were cramped, family upon family, into the courts off such streets. Because of the poor sanitation and the condition of the houses, disease was rife.

NOW: Ever-increasing demands of transport, accessibility and hygiene in the city saw many of its ancient lanes and slums cleared over the course of the twentieth century. Virtually all of old Wellington Lane has been demolished to make way for new housing. The section from Pottergate to St Benedict's, which was originally Duck Lane, is now also part of Wellington Lane.

THEN – CHAPEL FIELD DRILL HALL *c*1912: Opened in October 1866 by the Prince of Wales, the hall was built expressly for the use of the various volunteer and militia units based in the city. After the Haldane Reforms of 1907-8 it became the headquarters of the 4th Battalion, the Norfolk Regiment, which was part of the new territorial force. At this hall, thousands of soldiers, many of them territorials, volunteered for service in both the First and Second World Wars.

NOW: The drill hall, having survived the Luftwaffe's bombing raids, was taken down in 1963 to make way for the inner link road. During demolition parts of the old city wall were discovered.

CHAPEL FIELD GARDENS,

THEN – CHAPEL FIELD GARDENS *c***1910:** Before the pleasure gardens opened in 1880, there was a reservoir, with tower and pumping engines, on the site to feed higher parts of the city. Washerwomen used the pure water here and laid clean clothes out to dry on the grassy banks. The pagoda was an elaborate cast-iron pavilion designed by Thomas Jeckyll and made by local ironfounders Barnard, Bishop and Barnard, for the Philadelphia Exhibition of 1876.It was also shown at the Paris Exhibition of 1878. Norwich Corporation subsequently bought it for £500.

NOW: The iron pagoda was found to be unstable and was taken down in 1948, but the bandstand remains. Here there have been countless concerts from both military and civil bands, as well as performances by such entertainers as Marie Lloyd and even, according to local legend, Glenn Miller.

THEN – ST JOHN THE BAPTIST: Seen nearing completion in 1909, the Roman Catholic church of St John the Baptist was designed in the Early English style by George Gilbert Scott Junior and John Olrid Scott. It was built on the site of the city gaol, and was paid for by the generosity of the 15th Duke of Norfolk. Construction began in 1884 and the church was finished in 1912.

NOW: The completed church is 275ft long and 81ft high in the chancel, and it can seat a congregation of around 750. St John's occupies a commanding position near the site of the old St Giles Gates. The roadway has been replaced by a pedestrian walkway over Grapes Hill. The church was given cathedral status by the Vatican on March 13, 1976, and its first bishop was enthroned on June 2 of that year.

THEN – EARLHAM ROAD *c*1907: A drover, his dog and his whoppin' boy drive sheep from the market while the number 10 tram waits patiently behind, with yet another tram in the background. The scene is completed by the boy on the left with his trade 'barra'. On the right is The Black Horse public house, decked with posters advertising the Whit Tuesday Sports at Old Lakenham.

NOW: Gone are the trams, their lines and tracks, gone are the days of the cattle market near the castle and certainly long gone are the drovers and their livestock. Even the line of shops beside The Black Horse has now disappeared.

THEN – UNTHANK ROAD *c*1910: Viewed from the corner of Trinity Street, Unthank Road was one of the first developed beyond the old city walls in the nineteenth century. It takes its name from William Unthank (1760-1837), a local solicitor and property speculator. This and many other roads between Trinity Street and Mount Pleasant were built on the former Heigham House estate.

NOW: The gas lamps have been replaced by electric street lights, the tram wires and tracks are gone and the old Park Tavern is now called the Lillie Langtry.

THEN – BRUNSWICK ROAD *c*1912: Pictured in the days when even the postmen paused for the camera, Brunswick Road – no doubt because of its proximity to the Norfolk and Norwich Hospital – was lined with the homes and consulting rooms of many private physicians, and with the hospital's Private Patients' Home.

NOW: The left side remains almost the same, but the right has been swept away along with Shadwell Street and Nicholas Street for the development of the Norfolk and Norwich Hospital. A car park for hospital visitors is now on the site of the neat row of villas.

THEN – NEWMARKET ROAD *c*1911: This road was part of the first turnpike that linked the city with South Norfolk and, eventually, London. In this postcard the number 37 tram proceeds up the road towards the junction with Ipswich and Grove Roads.

NOW: Newmarket Road remains a busy entrance route to the city and has been streamlined over the years. The trees which lined the road towards the site of St Stephen's Gates have been removed for road widening.

THEN – NORFOLK AND NORWICH HOSPITAL: The hospital, founded in 1770, and built to designs by William Ivory, was completed in 1775. A further wing was added in 1802. In 1882 the hospital was rebuilt, with the foundation stone being laid by the then Prince of Wales. The total cost of this new hospital, inclusive of furnishings, was £57,116.

NOW: The hospital is about to be replaced by a new one outside the city at Colney. The magnificent frontage of the old hospital will be preserved, but the tower block of wards and the intrusive chimney will be demolished. Their sites will be used for domestic housing.

THEN – BOILEAU MEMORIAL AND FOUNTAIN *c*1910: This brick tower, at the junction of Ipswich and Newmarket Roads, had four arches, four pediments and a pyramidal roof. Inside were the figures of a woman and child designed by Sir Joseph Edgar Boehm in 1874. It was erected by Sir John Boileau as a memorial to his wife, Catherine. The statue was entitled Charity.

NOW: Traffic lights festoon the old junction. The brick tower was demolished in the 1950s to make way for road improvements and the figures of the woman and child were removed to the grounds of the Norfolk and Norwich Hospital in 1967, where they may still be seen, although almost totally obscured by foliage today.

THEN – GROVE ROAD *c*1907: A classic suburban street of early artisans' dwellings, built outside the city wall in the middle to late nineteenth century. Here the better paid workers could escape the cramped slums of the inner city but still be within walking distance or tram ride of their places of work.

NOW: Most of the houses on the left have been demolished and replaced by new town houses. It is interesting to note that the greater availability of private cars now makes vehicle-free images of such streets a near impossibility.

THEN – VICTORIA STATION *c*1910: Ceremonially opened in 1849, this station served passengers travelling from London on the Ipswich line. Within two years a new rail link enabled trains on this line to use the more commodious Thorpe Station instead.

NOW: Some local services continued to work in and out of Victoria Station until, in 1916, it was given over totally to goods. In this guise it saw another half century of service. The offices and car park of the Marsh insurance group now occupy the site of the passenger station.

THEN – ST STEPHEN'S STREET *c*1906: This was once one of the city's most popular shopping streets. Along its length were, to name but a few, Bunting's the outfitters; Lambert's, tea merchants; Duff, Morgan and Vermont, motor works; the Norwich Co-Operative Society and Brenner's Bazaar. There were also at least six public houses.

NOW: The charm of the old street has been destroyed by the joint contribution of the Luftwaffe's bombing raids, and road wideners. St Stephen's remains a popular centre for shopping with well-known local and national stores. Pedestrians may now even walk under part of its length by using the St Stephen's roundabout underpass.

THE OLD BOAR'S HEAD, NORWICH.

THEN – THE BOAR'S HEAD *c*1930: This building, on the corner of Surrey Street and St Stephen's Street, dated back to the mid-fifteenth century and was once the home of city alderman Richard Brown. In the seventeenth and eighteenth centuries it was known as The Greyhound, but was renamed Boar's Head after the heraldic device featured in the arms of the Norgate family who owned the pub and displayed their arms over the door in the 1790s.

NOW: The Boar's Head is remembered as a popular farmers' pub, where countryfolk gathered to mardle on market days until April 1942, when it was burned to a shell during a Baedeker raid. The pub was rebuilt after the war but not in the same style. Its character lost, it never enjoyed the same popularity again and the ground floor was converted into shop units, with offices above, in the St Stephen's road widening and development scheme of the late 1960s.

St. Stephen's Street, Norwich

THEN – ST STEPHEN'S STREET *c*1920: Viewed from St Stephen's Plain, this area was where the narrow old streets of Westlegate, Red Lion Street, Rampant Horse Street and St Stephen's met in a triangulated plain. Change and improvement was constant; Buntings, on the right, demolished its old warren of buildings for a grand new department store. The company advertised itself as 'draper, outfitter, boot and shoe specialist, silk mercer, carpet and manchester warehousemen'.

NOW: The road was widened during the 1950s and 1960s. Buntings was badly damaged in a fire bomb blitz in 1942, and moved to London Street next to Garlands. The store became a NAAFI with theatre, ballroom, dining hall, tavern and writing room. The neo-classical facade of architect Augustus Scott's building, one of the first to use reinforced concrete, was saved and today the store is occupied by Marks and Spencer.

THEN – THE THEATRE ROYAL: This was built in 1758, by Thomas Ivory, as a concert hall. Ten years later it was licensed as a theatre. Early in the nineteenth century the original building was demolished and the new Theatre Royal opened on March 27, 1826. In 1903 it was sold to Bostock and Fitt and its name changed to the Hippodrome. But Bostock and Fitt were also responsible for the Grand Opera House in St Giles Street. When, a few years later, variety and music hall became the vogue, the Grand Opera House became the Hippodrome and the Theatre Royal resumed its old name under a new proprietor, Fred Morgan.

NOW: The theatre was destroyed by fire on June 22, 1934, when most of its buildings were razed to the ground. Completely rebuilt, it re-opened on September 30, 1935. The theatre was refurbished and modernised in 1971, and again in the early 1990s.

THEN – ALL SAINTS' GREEN *c*1915: Some of these old buildings, on the eastern side of All Saints' Green, dated back to the sixteenth century. The house with the projecting bays and thatched roof was known as the Thatched Assembly Rooms. In 1915 it became the Thatched Cinema, which closed in 1930.

NOW: The cinema was purchased by RH Bond to adjoin his existing store as a restaurant, ballroom and furnishing showroom. This, along with most of the buildings on the east side of the green, was destroyed during the fire bombing of the city on June 27, 1941. Today the site is occupied entirely by the John Lewis store currently known as Bonds.

THEN – ORFORD PLACE *c*1905: This area owes much of its appearance to the architectural work of George Skipper. In the late nineteenth and early twentieth centuries the tumbledown properties in Red Lion Street were cleared in favour of fashionable new shops and apartments. The installation of the tram system knocked down many more of the old shops between The Bell and Back of the Inns.

NOW: The pediment on top of the Orford Arms has been lost, but the basic shape of the buildings on that side remain. In the background the grand old Norman Castle can be seen undergoing an £11 million refurbishment. Castle Meadow, beyond, is now closed to all but buses and taxis.

THEN – LAMB INN *c***1905:** All loaded up and ready for the off from the yard of the Lamb Inn is one of the four regular carriers that used the pub as a collection area for rounds serving many of the villages in the south of the county at the turn of the century. The Lamb is one of the oldest inns in the city, and its history includes a grisly murder in 1787, flooding in 1843, a miraculous escape from fire in 1939, a near miss during the blitz of 1941 and the untimely death of a wall-of-death stunt rider who fell from the roof in 1972.

NOW: Norwich has not escaped the vogue for changing the old-established names of pubs. Among casualties are the Lawyer, which is now the Fugitive and Ferkin, and the ancient Mischief Tavern, now known simply as the Mischief. The Lamb Inn is now graced with the title of Rat and Parrot.

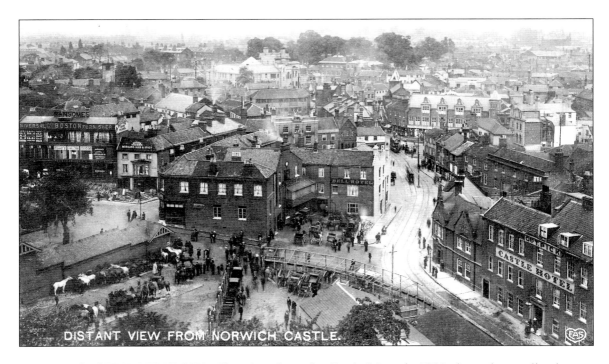

DISTANT VIEW FROM NORWICH CASTLE.

THEN – CASTLE MEADOW: The view from the Castle Mound *c*1902 shows horses lined up to be sold at Spellman's Horse Sale in the Castle Ditches. Beyond, all manner of carts are seen in front of the Bell Hotel. The new force on the road was the tram system, opened in July 1900; its construction involved demolition of shops between The Bell and Back of the Inns.

NOW: Much of the old view has been lost. The Horse Sale has gone the same way as the rest of the old cattle market site to become the Castle Mall. The fine old shop front of Curls, beyond in Orford Place, was destroyed in the blitz; later in the war the site held a reserve water supply for firefighters. Today the Curls site and those of other nearby bomb-damaged buildings are occupied by modern department stores and office blocks.

THEN – CASTLE MEADOW II: This 1948 picture shows how Castle Meadow looked before the building of the Castle Mall shopping precinct, when the car park and wall were demolished in 1990. Some of the trees shown here were blown down during the October 1987 hurricane.

NOW: A £11 million refurbishment programme is currently being carried out on Castle Museum. This includes a lift from Castle Meadow to the top of the mound. Castle Meadow is now a very much quieter thoroughfare, used only by buses and taxis.

THEN – CASTLE MEADOW III *c*1958: In the centre of the line of shops is the entrance to the Castle Hotel which, at the turn of the nineteenth and twentieth centuries, occupied the whole block.

NOW: The shops and hotel were demolished for the Castle Mall and Castle Meadow redevelopment of the 1990s. Castle Meadow access is now limited to buses and city taxis.

THEN – CATTLE MARKET STREET *c*1906: The street, which leads from Rose Lane to Golden Ball Street, is seen before its surface was made up, and while in this state in the autumn and winter months, it became a slippery mire caused by the livestock being driven to and from the market – which is seen on the right. In summer time, the cattle threw up great clouds of dust.

NOW: The road has been macadamed and vehicles replace the cattle. All of the auctioneers' and merchants' offices have gone and to the right the foliage-covered walls of Castle Mall and gardens occupy the site of the stalls of the old cattle market.

THEN – AGRICULTURAL HALL 1914: Troops of the Essex Regiment, complete with their supply waggons, stop for a wash and brush-up in front of the hall. The hall, opened in 1882, saw grand exhibitions, theatrical performances, political rallies and trade shows as well as the popular fat stock shows. There was even a roller skating rink inside.

NOW: In the late 1950s Anglia Television acquired the building from Norwich Corporation on a seventy-five-year lease, and it was included in the complex of buildings which includes offices and studios for Anglia.

THEN – AGRICULTURAL HALL PLAIN *c*1905: To the right is the Agricultural Hall, which gave its name to the Plain. Next door is the grand Bath stone building erected by Sir Robert Harvey as the Crown Bank, opened in 1866. After the collapse of the bank the building became the city's General Post Office.

NOW: Both the post office and the Agricultural Hall have been absorbed into the Anglia Television complex. The building on the left was the Royal Hotel, built 1896-97. Over the last fifty years it has housed a variety of businesses and is now undergoing a refit to become a business centre known as The Royal.

THEN – PRINCE OF WALES ROAD *c*1925: All manner of businesses and offices were set up on this busy access route to the city. On the left, beyond the Norfolk Dairy Farmers' Association, is Backs, the leading vintner in the city in its day. Backs also ran the Curat House on The Haymarket where staff did their own bottling, The Grapes public house on Wensum Street and another shop on Exchange Street.

NOW: Gone are all traces of the old tram system, and the traction columns seen in the 1925 photograph have been replaced by street lamp standards. Most of the old offices have also gone, to be replaced by restaurants, shops and estate agents.

Prince of Wales Road Norwich. W.2033.

THEN – PRINCE OF WALES ROAD II: This animated view of 1906 shows the road when many of the developments were still considered 'new'. It was planned as a grand boulevard connecting the station and the city, but like many well-intentioned schemes it ran out of money. Alexandra Mansions at the top of the road was part of this plan. On the left, shops due for redevelopment can be seen. The building behind the tram was the old vinegar factory.

NOW: The boulevard development was never finished and the left side of the road had to wait for various speculators to demolish and replace the old properties with new. The area to the right, which was covered in trees, is now the site for a large office block. The hoardings just in front of the block surround the site of a demolished old garage.

CARROW WORKS
NORWICH.

THEN – THE RIVER AND CARROW WORKS *c*1910: The name of Colman is synonymous with one of the city's most famous exports – mustard. Jeremiah James Colman founded the business in 1805 in an old mill at Stoke Holy Cross. The Carrow Works was built in 1856, giving closer access to road, rail and river transport. At this time more than 3,000 employees worked here where mustard was produced along with starch, laundry blue and cornflour.

NOW: The old Carrow Bridge was demolished in 1922. It was replaced by a new one, opened by the Prince of Wales in 1923, further up the river. The Carrow Works still operates today but only mustard is produced from the old catalogue. The name of Colman has survived a number of takeovers and buy-outs.

THEN – THORPE STATION: The impressive brick building under a zinc dome was the work of Norwich builders, J Youngs and Son, and it opened in 1888. The first stationmaster was George Jessup, who later became Superintendent of the Great Eastern Railway's Norfolk district.

NOW: The station has been restored to its pre-war look by Railtrack. Today no cars are allowed to use the main gates; vehicle access is via the new Riverside development off to the right of the picture. The photographer was able to capture here one of the city's few remaining pony and traps.

THEN – RIVERSIDE: The Great Eastern Hotel on the left was demolished in the 1960s to make way for the new Hotel Nelson. The tug *Terrible*, owned by J Hobrough & Son, is seen going under Foundry Bridge with her funnel lowered. She is towing a wherry, which has been stripped of her mast, gaff and sail and which was probably used for carrying mud dredged from the riverbed.

NOW: The Hotel Nelson is on the left and in the centre, through the bridge, the Norwich Yacht Basin may be glimpsed – a popular mooring place in the summer months. On the right is a floating restaurant in a converted coaster.

THEN – PULL'S FERRY *c*1906: One of the most photographed landmarks of the city, here Pull's Ferry is seen from the Cathedral precincts rather than from the more usual Riverside viewpoint. This ancient water gate was built in the fifteenth century over the canal which was cut from the river up to Cathedral Close. The canal was filled in during the latter half of the eighteenth century but the ferry service remained.

NOW: The gatehouse and the pub beside it fell into disrepair from the early nineteenth century, and was described as 'the roughest bit of picturesque Norwich' at one time. The ferry ceased to run in 1930. The site was sympathetically restored in the 1950s with money raised by Norwich Girl Guides.

THEN – BISHOP BRIDGE *c*1905: A bridge has been recorded here since the thirteenth century. This one was built by Richard Spynk between 1337 and 1341 and once had a large gatehouse on top to form part of the city's defensive wall. In the foreground is the 30-ton wherry *Charles Henry,* one of hundreds of such craft which were familiar sights along this waterway when the photograph was taken.

NOW: In 1923 the bridge was identified as one which should be widened. This would have meant its certain destruction, but fortunately a group of concerned citizens got together to form the Norwich Society, and managed to save it. Increased traffic in the latter half of the twentieth century threatened its survival. It has now been preserved from further such damage by being closed to cars and lorries. Only pedestrians and cyclists may cross it today.

ST. PAUL'S CHURCH NORWICH

THEN – ST PAUL'S CHURCH *c*1908: One of the few round tower churches in Norwich, St Paul's was a charming mix of Norman, Decorated and Perpendicular periods. It was just off Barrack Street in St Paul's Square, by the junction with Peacock Street. The church was restored and a chancel added in 1870. In 1882 the churchyard was laid out as a garden by John Gurney.

NOW: St Paul's Church was gutted by fire when incendiaries and high explosive bombs destroyed large areas of the city on June 27, 1942. Today the remains of the church, together with most of the area it served, are under the inner link road.

THEN – MAGDALEN STREET *c*1910: The view is from the Magdalen Gates and shows the street when it was still one of the most popular shopping areas in the city. The name Magadalen is comparatively modern, and is derived from the chapel nearby. Until well into the nineteenth century it was known as Fybrigge Street.

NOW: By the 1950s the demographic changes in the city brought on the closure of the boot and shoe factories in the area, and the popularity of the shopping centre diminished. In 1959 the street was given a face-lift with the help of the Civic Trust, but much of the good work was lost in 1971 when the inner link road was ploughed through and over the street.

THEN – STUMP CROSS *c*1912: A rare picture showing, from left to right, a coffee house and grocery, the entrance to Elephant Yard, the Elephant public house (owned by Steward and Patteson), the entrance to Bishop's Court, a stationers, another grocery and tea dealer and a post office.

NOW: The buildings on the previous page were demolished in 1971 to make way for the Magdalen Street flyover. Behind this is the Anglia Square shopping centre.

THEN – COLEGATE *c*1909: Looking westwards towards Duke Street, this view shows The Black Boys Inn on the left. Off the yard beside the pub the Glover sisters ran a small school in the mid-nineteenth century. Sarah Ann Glover taught singing with her own unique method – the tonic sol-fa which has now become the adopted way to teach singing all over the world. Just beyond that was Howlett and White's boot and shoe factory, at the time one of the biggest manufacturers of its kind in the city.

NOW: In the 1990s the name of the pub became 'politically incorrect' and it was changed to The Merchants of Colegate. Howlett and White, known in later years as Norvic Shoes, closed and is now an office complex for Norwich Union. On the right is the beamed Bacon's House, named after a mid-sixteenth century mayor of Norwich who lived there. Today it is the headquarters of the Norwich Society.

THEN – ROSEMARY LANE *c*1910:
The lane takes its name from the old Pilgrim's Hall which was converted into the Rosemary Tavern. The scene is viewed from St Mary's Plain towards St Miles' Alley when it was a little street of tenements, some of which dated back to the sixteenth century.

NOW: Much of the lane was demolished during the slum clearance programme of the 1930s. Bomb damage put paid to all the rest, except for Pykerell's House. This was owned by Norfolk Archaeological Trust and was lovingly restored after the war. The house was built in the sixteenth century by city sheriff and mayor, Thomas Pykerell, and became Pilgrims Hall and subsequently Rosemary Tavern.

Elm Hill, Norwich

THEN – ELM HILL *c*1933: In the centre of the picture is the distinctive gable of the Briton's Arms, and in the foreground, to the left, is Robert Townshend's antiques shop. It is difficult to imagine that just a handful of years before this idyllic view was captured, Elm Hill had been declared a slum area. It was saved from demolition by just one councillor's carrying vote.

NOW: Elm Hill remains the gem of streets in the city's historic 'crown'. Thousands every year visit its eclectic selection of shops housed in some of the best-preserved old properties in the city. Here you will find antiques and collectables, jewellery and crafts.

THEN – COWGATE STREET *c*1907:
A century ago Cowgate ran from Magdalen Street to Whitefriars Bridge (the road from the bridge to St Martin's Plain was Whitefriars). The name Cowgate is derived from the Saxon *cowholme*, which means cow island, for it was here that the ancient citizens of Norwich grazed their cattle.

NOW: Cowgate, now Whitefriars, has been bisected by the Magdalen Street fly-over, and the narrow little street with its smart cobblestoned surface, and well made gutters, has mostly been demolished to make way for a road-widening scheme and modern houses.

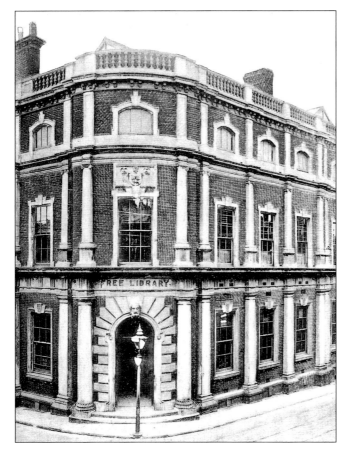

THEN – THE PUBLIC LIBRARY: The library was built at the corner of St Andrew and Duke Streets for £10,000, and it opened in 1857. Over the years it was enlarged to accommodate more than 22,000 books, some 10,000 local-interest pamphlets and around 7,000 local maps, portraits and views in its reference section. The lending library – open every day of the week – was just as impressive, with about 20,000 volumes on its shelves.

NOW: The old building closed in 1963 and the books were moved to a new library in Bethel Street. There, many of the historic treasures in the local studies department were destroyed by fire in August 1994. The original building was taken down to make way for the car park seen here, and the telephone exchange.

THEN – CHARING CROSS *c*1908: The name Charing Cross is a corruption of Shearing Cross, a reflection of the wool trade so prominent in the city during the mediæval period. Here St Andrew's Street divides into St Benedict's Street on the left, and Westwick Street on the right. Until the 1890s the divide and widths of these streets were much narrower. The building in the centre was the city office of Mapperley Colliery, whose depot was at the City Station. It replaced an earlier structure three times as wide, which for many years was a public house called The Three Pigeons.

NOW: The modern divide made at the turn of the nineteenth and twentieth centuries remains much the same as does the Victorian gable end to the dividing building. The shops in this area have, however, changed dramatically, as specialist collectors' shops and musical instrument showrooms fill most of St Benedict's Street.

THEN – BOTOLPH STREET *c*1910: This was named after the long-dissolved church of St Boltolph which stood nearby. The street was once a busy shopping area between St Augustine's and Magdalen Street. When this photograph was taken Botolph Street had five pubs, a girls' home, eleven yards and thirty-nine shops and businesses.

NOW: Botolph Street was once home to a number of well-remembered Norwich shops, like Frank Price, to the original Odeon cinema and Robert's printing business. All were swept away in the 1971 redevelopment scheme. In their place are the Anglia Square shopping centre, a new Odeon cinema and Sovereign House, home to Her Majesty's Stationery Office for more than twenty years.

Midland and Great Northern (City) Station, Norwich.

2621. 17.

THEN – NORWICH CITY STATION: This terminus was built next to the river Wensum, half-a-mile north west of the city centre. Its red brick facade was broken by pilasters of yellow brick, each capped to resemble carved stone. Through the arch lay two long, canopied platforms. The station was wrecked by enemy bombing in 1941 and a small prefabricated building was put up in its place.

NOW: This roundabout, constructed in the early 1970s, stands on the site of the old City Station. Halfords motor centre is in the background and the road to the left (Barker Street) has various retail outlets. The road to the right, St Crispin's Road, leads to Magdalen Street flyover and forms part of the Norwich inner ring road.

DEREHAM ROAD NORWICH

THEN – DEREHAM ROAD *c*1910: This view is taken looking towards the city centre. The shop on the left belongs to CW Clarke, and further down on the same side is the turning into Exeter Street. The Lord John Russell public house is on the right. A good reference point is the church of St Lawrence, where there is a spirelet on the north east angle of the tower.

NOW: Cars have replaced the trams, horses and carts and it is no longer safe to walk in the centre of this road. On the left is Raglan Street, and the large building, formerly the Regal Cinema, is now a public house called The City Gate. In the background is the junction with Barn Road and Grapes Hill. St Lawrence's church may still be seen in the far distance.

ABOUT THE AUTHOR

Philip Standley was born in Wymondham and has lived there all his life. He spent his working life in the family's television and hardware retail business. His main hobby is collecting postcards, mainly of Wymondham and Norwich, and he was a founder member of Norfolk Postcard Club. His first book, *Norwich in Old Picture Postcards*, was published in 1988 and was followed by three further volumes. He also assisted in the production of two books on local railways.

ABOUT THE PHOTOGRAPHER

Terry Burchell was born in Kent and has lived in Norfolk on and off for thirty-six years, working mainly in the printing industry and finally as a print ordering officer with HMSO before his retirement. He has been involved in photography for as long as he could hold a camera, both as an amateur and later as a freelance professional. Much of the work he undertakes now is for museums and libraries, copying old photographs and documents.